AESOPEAN

AESOPEAN

W.D. JACKSON

with eight woodcuts by Alan Dixon

Shoestring Press

Printed by imprintdigital
Upton Pyne, Exeter
www.digital.imprint.co.uk

Typesetting and cover design by The Book Typesetters
hello@thebooktypesetters.com
07422 598 168
www.thebooktypesetters.com

Published by Shoestring Press
19 Devonshire Avenue, Beeston, Nottingham, NG9 1BS
(0115) 925 1827
www.shoestringpress.co.uk

First published 2022
© Copyright text: W.D. Jackson
© Copyright illustrations: Alan Dixon
© Cover illustration: Alan Dixon

The moral right of the author has been asserted.

ISBN 978-1-915553-17-1

ACKNOWLEDGEMENTS

Sections from *Aesopean (1) & (2)* first appeared in *Acumen*, *The Fortnightly Review*, *Poetry Salzburg Review*.

The pamphlet owes a considerable debt to Laura Gibbs, *Aesop's Fables* (2002), in particular to its 'Introduction' and excellent 'General Index'.

AESOPEAN (1)

"Aesop the storyteller, our great benefactor, happened to be a slave…"
– *Life of Aesop*, Anon. (1st century, AD)

i

A herdsman showed his quarrelling sons
How hard it is to bend
A well-bound bundle, which – in ones
Or twos – will break in the end.

His neighbour, a merchant, ignored the sticks
But with bundles could always turn
A profit. Or play dirty tricks –
For example, bundles burn.

ii

A poor wild ass inquired of his friend,
A donkey, *how* he'd grown so plump.
The donkey grinned. But his backbone was bent
From the stones he had to hump.

The ass, sneering, chewed a dry thistle.
That night a starving pack
Of hyenas chewed *him*, skin and gristle.
The donkey rested his back.

iii

Winter. A hungry cicada begged
A colony of ants for food...
– *All summer we gathered grain, thin-legged*
Though we are. You sang. What good

Was that? We worked, you played. It's wrong
To think that God will provide...
But St Francis praised the cicada's song –
And when he died it died.

iv

Before the cat was belled, the mice
Were all for one, one all.
Their elders' sound but unheeded advice
Was *Hide – and* let *her prowl...*

After, they gave up helping each other
And squabbled: which male got more
Females / space / food? And which big brother
Should lead them into war?

v

Enemy soldiers approached a farm –
"Let's leg it," the farmer said
To his donkey, who pondered: *What's the harm?*
I'll work for them *instead.*

I've got two panniers and four good hooves,
I'm sound in mind and limb.
But the enemy army was short of food,
And so they butchered him.

vi

The fox was gone: the grapes still hung
Too high for him to reach.
The Bremen Musicians chanced along:
The cock plucked bunches each.

He liked green grapes. The donkey tried
A few, then munched some hay.
The cat and dog, though, ate them and died.
The fox came back next day.

vii

A vain old vixen had never seen
A lion, until one day
She saw one big enough to dine
On her – and slunk away.

No roar pursued her. They met again –
The lion yawned. When, later,
She dared to hobnob, he shook his mane,
Pounced on her back, and ate her.

viii

(after Goethe)

One winter a mob of frogs – imprisoned
Deep in a frozen pool –
Promised, *If spring returns to free us*
We'll set ourselves to school

Among the leaves and learn to sing
Like nightingales! Spring came.
They paired in the mud – croaked – spawned off-spring,
Sated with more of the same.

ix

One night a fisherman's net was full
Of a large and various catch.
Smart small-fry slipped away. Big dull
Flounders went down the hatch.

A monstrous shark, though, scenting blood,
Snapped up the shoal, capsized
The vessel. Fish and men, as food
For sharks, are any-sized.

x

(after Grimms' Märchen, *No.75)*

A cat encountered a sleek fox
Behind the old Manor Farm
Where recently six at least of the cock's
Dumb wives had come to harm.

You know a lot of tricks, my friend,
She grinned as she shinned up a tree –
I one. But the farmer's hounds, in the end,
Will tear you to bits, not me.

xi

(after Goethe)

An old and toothless lion invited
The fox and stork to dinner.

A long-necked vase with fish provided
The best of meals for the thinner.

Chicken (not grapes) on a golden platter
Flattered the somewhat fatter.

Each mocked the other's ill-bred manners.
But the lion was no one's fool.

The old being nothing if not planners,
His plan was – *Divide and rule.*

xii

(after Heine)

There are two common sorts of rat:
One hungry and one fat.
The fat rats stay content at home;
The thin and hungry roam.

From continent to continent,
Nothing on earth can, now, prevent
Their progress – nothing sate
Their need to find more things to eat.

*

Their litters swell great nameless groups:
Females are common property.
Their stubborn, rat-radical, foul-mouthed troops
Know nothing of Christianity.

They file on grimly, straight ahead –
Cross mountains, deserts, seas.
If any fall, they're left for dead.
The living carry disease.

*

The fat rats only think of guzzling,
Though some fall prey to sozzling.
While sozzling and guzzling, they do not think
Of the legions of skinny rats on the brink

Of doing the *sort* of damage that
The biggest, wildest, hungriest cat
Could not conceive of. By changing the rules,
They make the wise look fools.

AESOPEAN (2)

"... a rat is not an elephant"
– Jean de la Fontaine, *Fables* VIII, 15

i

(after Lessing)

A goose there was whose feathers shone
So white she wondered if
She had in fact been born a swan...
Her neck, it's true, was stiff –
And too short, perhaps? When on her own,
She strove to stretch and curve it.
And swanned about the lake alone.
Her flock-mates honked to observe it.

ii

(after Lessing)

An ostrich boomed, *I wanna fly!*
And raced as fast as he could
Across the plain, beneath the sky –
The fastest of any bird.

He ran so hard he lost his breath:
With one last desperate bound
He briefly soared to a hero's death
And smashed into the ground.

iii

A frog swam into a shallow pool
And fell asleep. The sun
Heated the lakeside slowly. *Fool!*
An adder hissed: *No fun
For me, though, if you don't survive! –*
And slept as well. The lake
Grew hotter. The frog awoke – and lived.
An eagle ate the snake.

iv

(after Lessing)

Bones, skin and putrid flesh were all
Of a hero's famous war-horse
That remained, after a fatal fall,
While Nature ran her course.

A swarm of wasps had made their nest
Inside this rotting beast –
Whose glorious history was their boast,
Whose carcass their fixed feast.

(Heine, "Ein Fichtenbaum steht einsam")

In the North a lonely fir-tree
On a barren mountain height
Slumbers, benumbed by blankets
Of ice-and-snowy white.

He dreams of a sunlit palm-tree
In the farthest East of all –
Where she grieves, alone and silent
On a scorching rocky wall.

vi

(after Lessing)

Beneath a massive oak-tree, a pig –
Eyes glued to the leaf-strewn ground –
Ate acorn after acorn. Big
And smart – though muddy – he grubbed all round.

Tall branches waved in the autumn wind:
Ungrateful brute, hissed the tree.
The pig kept munching, grunted, grinned:
You didn't drop 'em for me!

vii

A lion, enraged with his partner, a wolf,
For having the nerve to divide
Their prey in equal parts, engulfed
His head with a roar. The wolf died.

Their fellow-hunter, a fox, to appease
His Highness, begged to suggest
He eat what he liked. The lion, pleased,
Allowed him to feast on the rest.

16

viii

A raven found a lump of cheese
And perched with it in her beak
On a branch. A dog-fox wheedled, *Please,*
Mrs Crow, you look so sleek –

With your beak so strong and pointed – won't
You sing for me – I know
You can, o Queen of the Birds – I can't
Wait for a song or two...

*

The fox's wife spoke next. The serene
Raven still held her lump
Of Cheddar. *Call yourself a Queen?*
She sneered. *You sad old frump!...*

But the raven paid no serious heed
To the praise or blame of such
Sly (self-) deceivers – who shortly agreed
They'd never liked cheese much.

ix

A lion had caught a hare when a stag
Ran by. The hare cried, *Lunch,*
Your Majesty! – A BIGGER bag
Of bones for you to crunch!!

– Don't move, the lion growled – and followed
The fleet-footed stag. Hares hide
With ease. The greedy lion swallowed
Nothing that day but his pride.

x

A bull dropped so much dung on a field
The mice who lived there too
Thought up a plan to try and shield
Their holes from his pats of poo:

When he raised his tail, one ran out and bit
His nose – ran in – repeated
The process. The roaring bull, plus bullshit,
Angrily – helplessly – retreated.

xi

A badly treated slave complained
To Aesop that his master
Beat him for nothing. Aesop explained
That blows would rain the faster
If he *did* something, such as try
To run away. Blows rained
On the slave as before: "It's do or die,"
He decided. Ventured. And gained.

(after Tommaso da Celano)

St Francis praised a flock of birds
For joyfully praising their Maker
In beautiful song, as he with words:
"Gratitude turns a taker
Into an open-hearted giver,
My sisters: you neither sow
Nor reap – praise, praise the wind and weather,
And all things here below!

Be praised, with all Your creatures, Lord:
We thank You for our Mother the Earth
Who supports and feeds us, bringing forth
Her berries and fruits, her trees and grass.

Be praised for Brother Wind – for the air
And constantly changing weather,
Cloudy and cool or soft and fair! –
Where all things change and pass."

NOTES

Aesopean (1)

p. 1, *Aesop the storyteller etc.:* The historical Aesop may well have been a Greek-speaking slave, later freedman, living in Phrygia in the fifth or sixth century BC. Some of the fables as we know them were first written down by Latin and Greek authors from the first century AD onwards – and have been translated or adapted into other languages up to the present. It is only in a limited sense, therefore, that short tales of this sort – whose roots and ramifications are practically endless – can be viewed as the work of any one author. The latest version is no more, or less, than the latest version.

p. 2, *But St Francis praised the cicada's song:* For eight days shortly before his death in 1226, St Francis is said to have been visited every morning outside his cell at the Portiuncula chapel near Assisi by a cicada, which sang for him (St Bonaventure, *The Life of St Francis*, ch.8): cp. note on p. 20, "(after Tommaso da Celano)".

Aesopean (2)

p. 12, *"a rat is not an elephant":* In La Fontaine's fable *(ca.* 1678) a rat mocks a majestic elephant, bearing along a Queen with her cat, dog and other accoutrements. The rat asks why observers should praise mere *size*. Marianne Moore, in her superlative *Fables of La Fontaine* (1952), translates:

'Who cares how much space something occupies?'
He said. 'Size does not make a thing significant!
All crowding near an elephant? Why must I worship him?
Servile to brute force at which mere tots might faint?
Should persons such as I admire his heavy limb?
    I pander to an elephant!'
    About to prolong his soliloquy

When the cat broke from captivity
And instantly proved what her victim would grant:
That a rat is not an elephant.

p. 12, *(after Lessing):* The pre-Romantic dramatist, poet and critic, G.E. Lessing (1729–81) based most of his mainly prose fables on early Greek and Latin authors – for example, the Augustan poet Phaedrus, whose common sense appealed to his Enlightenment values. Goethe's and Heine's contributions to the Aesopean tradition came somewhat later. Both poets suffered in their earlier works from Romantic attitudes of various sorts, from which they may be said to have recovered in different ways.

p. 21, *(after Tommaso da Celano):* Tommaso completed the earliest biography of the saint in 1229. He certainly knew St Francis in person, becoming a Franciscan monk in 1215, shortly after the order was founded. Ch. XXI of his book is entitled 'Of his preaching to the birds and of the obedience of the creatures'. Other stories of Francis resemble Aesopean fables – for example, 'How St Francis converted the very fierce wolf of Gubbio' *(The Little Flowers of St Francis,* ch. XXI) – adapted in my *Opus 3* as *'Al Vescovo d'Assisi'.* The second and third stanzas of xii are adapted from St Francis' famous 'Canticle of Brother Sun', also in *Opus 3.*

Alan Dixon's woodcut on the front cover was quite likely his first – exhibited in 1960 at a print exhibition in the AIA Gallery. Shoestring Press published his *73 Woodcuts* in 2011 and an exhibition of prints at the Redfern Gallery was held to coincide with the launch there of his most recent collection of poems, *The Wall Dancer*, Shoestring Press, 2017. His first collection was published by the Fortune Press in 1964. Others, including *The Seaweed's Secret*, twenty of his poems by Max Jacob, have been published by Poet & Printer, Redbeck Press, Spectacular Diseases, and Shoestring Press. He was born in Waterloo, Lancashire, in 1936.

Further comments on *Opus 3*:

"With regard to *Opus 3*, one thinks of something which Dryden famously wrote in the Preface to his *Fables*... surveying the range and variety of Chaucer's achievement, he observes, "Tis sufficient to say, according to the Proverb, that here is God's Plenty'... 'Plenty' or abundance is not always or necessarily a virtue where poetry is concerned. But when poetry is as generous and as disciplined, both technically and intellectually, as *Opus 3* is, it deserves to be welcomed without qualification."
– Glyn Pursglove, *Poetry Salzburg Review*

"W.D. Jackson's *Opus 3* is an epic, a tour de force, a poetic endeavour that surpasses anything else to be seen in the contemporary literary landscape... It is unique, and the only comparable modern work is Ezra Pound's series of Cantos – except that the poetry in *Opus 3* is accessible and readable... The author shows a mastery of many styles of composition and verse-forms – the poetry is first rate." – Kevin Bailey, *HQ Magazine*

"A major poem of civilization and discontents... Layered and multifaceted... where it wins so often is in the sheer skill of the verse-making... This, like the preceding volumes, is an important addition to our cultural knowledge..." – Roland John, *Acumen*